What We Call Dances

Don Schaeffer

ISBN: 978-93-6354-935-7

First Edition: 2024
Rs. 200/-

Cyberwit.net
HIG 45 Kaushambi Kunj, Kalindipuram
Allahabad - 211011 (U.P.) India
http://www.cyberwit.net
Tel: +(91) 9415091004
E-mail: info@cyberwit.net

Printed at Repro India Limited.

Contents

A View of Knees

The hour hand
on the wall clock,
the big fancy one
shoved down,
covering the two,
and the light
from above somehow
dimmed. The ground
seemed to bend its knees
just a little. The breeze
made a sound
like a voice. It said,
“knee bends!”
I heard strange music
like knee bends
was a song.
Then
nothing was the same.
I had to sleep.

Awakeness

Our language came out in blocks.
Blocks is what we knew, a breath,
silence followed by articulation
which we could carry away.
But most was quick to
dissipate in the moving air.
Our dearest moments
alive in strings of shaking air
couldn't make it to our hearts.
The real beauty was in the taste
and in the content of our fingers.

We inherited habits of turning away,
leaving bare spots. Most of the
topology of time was bare.
There were just thickened
lumps of value. Those
got the names. The rest just passed.
And the world
became a string. We breathed
and squeezed in remnants of secrets
and left most of it
resting on the floor.

I remember love.

It was quiet,
staring hungrily at the future,
mostly aspiration and dream.
Quiet days when the
work was done and illusions
were checked, converted to
smiles and good deeds.
I don't think I could have
handled passion. It would have
converted to lies.
I remember the wishes,
the fantasies in the dark.
We kept each other alive with it.
We had educated hopes.

Here I Am

Every day
I check my existence
by counting the
the patterns of little dots.
A small chill of embarrassment
is my only real
reaction to what I see.

The thing is, I have learned
to make the embarrassment
into flattery. It warms the world
to luke warm and I can
live with that.

I love you real world,
even though I am not
always faithful. I rise
in the morning loving you
as if you were a person
who could return feelings.

The Cost

At three-forty-five in the afternoon,
he showed up.
And there was something
outlandish about his uniform,
which I'm sure I
wasn't supposéd to note.

He was an
immediate burden to my eyes,
costly to see. He drew
something out of me
and didn't pay.

He toured the room
but it did not raise my hopes.
His presence pulled hope
out of me, attached by a
string to time.

He left after an hour
without speaking.
He only
glanced at me with smiles,
and said "good day,"
which made it worse.

Icewater Dreams

After we are born
we are tossed into
puddles of icewater.
We can do it. We
have skin and hair.
They try to help us
but they really don't
want to and often
don't know how.

After we are born
we make up messages
that reassure us
but are often not true.
The big ones try to help
but are nearly drowned and
frozen themselves.

After we are born
we are lucky it's
not too cold. We secure
cloth and wriggle
to keep warm.
We call that
dances.

The Vascillating Distance

Do apes love children
like we love cats?
Would apes kill babies
without looking into their
little eyes? To apes,
are babies cute like kittens?
Have we come far enough and
are we going further?
The feel of fur
takes away the rage.
They let me touch them
for their safety but we
decline to do the same.

Takita Maluma (Whom I Owe to Wolfgang Kohler)

You are Takita.
So am I.
Maluma lives elsewhere.

Rehearsing

I have hidden under a mask of life
all my years, never met death in person.
I think at my first personal face-to-face meeting

I may be a player.

That doesn't mean I won't fear. I am afraid
of big and powerful things. This, nothing will
scare away. It is not capable of mercy.

A Pickle

I wanna
take my bongos
and go home.
I lost those bongos
a long time ago
and they vanished
even from humor
and the home too.
That leaves only
smiles and courage.
I don't like those.

Writing Poetry

When the poem slows me down
I breathe. I wait.
I see my neighbors
waiting for me to move.
But I can't. "Get out of the way"
they say. I try to roll over
in the rocks full of sand.
My way is small
I can't share it.
I don't know how
to share it. Trained to
be alone, my selfishness
is habit.

Brevity Is Wit

Did you know
that the trash can
was really a tube
that leads to the water channel
under the ground.
All the words
that end up there
are eaten by the earth.
The earth is a
silence factory.
All those words
fighting to be born,
starting beloved
pass and break up,
soundless. You know
the brief life of a word.

Oh The Day

I whistle a masterpiece.
The amplifier in my brain
is plugged in to recorder in my dreams.
You can see me
sailing over the floor,
eyes on the sky, arms
floating high over my head.
The princess of vain hope
is waiting below me in her
gown of neon. Oh me, I sing
at the future. And she
is already at the door
with bags packed.

Dreams I Don't Reveal

In the night quiet
I am nothing but wishes.
There are no walls here.
Time and silence
carve pathways like
rivulets through the dark.
I have the elements,
the ingredients from dreams.
Everything real has been removed,
snatched and carried away.
But there are many playful ghosts.
Time Is a vast hallway.
Memory is a toolkit.
Laughter is broken off the past.
Shiny shards are scattered
in the dark.

Expired Fate

It was the first
part of vìsion,
a sight
there was no time for.

I looked to the left
and she had turned away,
casting off the impulse.
Decades washed away.

Tens of futures,
crumbled. Time
staggered and nearly
fell. But I knew
in my knees,
it was
entirely right.

The Plan of Things

Do things plan to destroy each other?
Why can't things live in peace?
Protection is so one-sided and expensive.
The costs of the Earth are high.
Yet a peacful tangerine is greeted by
the fearsome mold and we are left without taste.
Doesn't fate care?

Constructive Hysteria

Foreign things,
strange things,
different visions
came back
in an accidental afternoon,
even late, when it should be over.
One constructive memory
remained, of little devils
made by children.
This dose of memory
persists.

Waking in the Middle of the Night

I know them from a distance.
But they are so familiar I would
even call them intimate. They
belong to me just as they
belong to you. And I can't
possess all the ones that I
didn't own before. Almost all
I will never touch. They are
shared but at such distance.
Created by chance that cold
mechanics excretes into the place
of sound and light but I
can't believe it. We even
call it "we" but it's nearly in jest.
There is such space between us.
Why are you shaped that way?
Where did you originate?
What do your vibrations signify?
When will we say goodbye?

Thw Studentless Teacher

He just longed for ears.
He had an empty voice
and lectured in an empty room.
He made
words that had no sound.
Patient watchers
decided how they would
ignore him. I don't fault them.
Time is costly and value is scarce.
Speech is also
the grandest pleasure,
easy to deliver
and costly to accept.

When I See My Neighbors

When the poem slows me down
I breathe. I wait.
I see my neighbors

waiting for me to move.
But I can't. "Get out of the way"
they say. I try to roll over

in the rocks full of sand.
My way is small
I can't share it.

I don't know how to share it.
Trained to be alone, my selfishness
is habit. I mean nothing by it.

The Cost

At three-forty-five in the afternoon,
he showed up.
And there was something
outlandish about his uniform,
which I'm sure I
wasn't supposéd to note.

He was an
immediate burden to my eyes,
costly to see. He drew
something out of me
and didn't pay.

He toured the room
but it did not raise my hopes.
His presence pulled hope
out of me, attached by a
string to time.

He left after an hour
without speaking.
He only
glanced at me with smiles,
and said "good day,"
which made it worse.

Rehearsing

I have hidden under a mask of life
all my years, never met death in person.
I think at my first personal face-to-face meeting

I may be a player.

That doesn't mean I won't fear. I am afraid
of big and powerful things. This, nothing will
scare away. It is not capable of mercy.

A Pickle

I wanna
take my bongos
and go home.
I lost those bongos
a long time ago
and they vanished
even from humor
and the home too.
That leaves only
smiles and courage.
I don't like those.

A View of Knees

The hour hand
on the wall clock,
the big fancy one
shoved down,
covering the two,
and the light
from above somehow
dimmed. The ground
seemed to bend its knees
just a little. The breeze
made a sound
like a voice. It said,
"knee bends!"
I heard strange music
like knee bends
was a song.
Then
nothing was the same.
I had to sleep.

www.ingramcontent.com/pod-product-compliance
Lightning Source LLC
LaVergne TN
LVHW041005150826
845672LV00002B/884

* 9 7 8 9 3 6 3 5 4 9 3 5 7 *